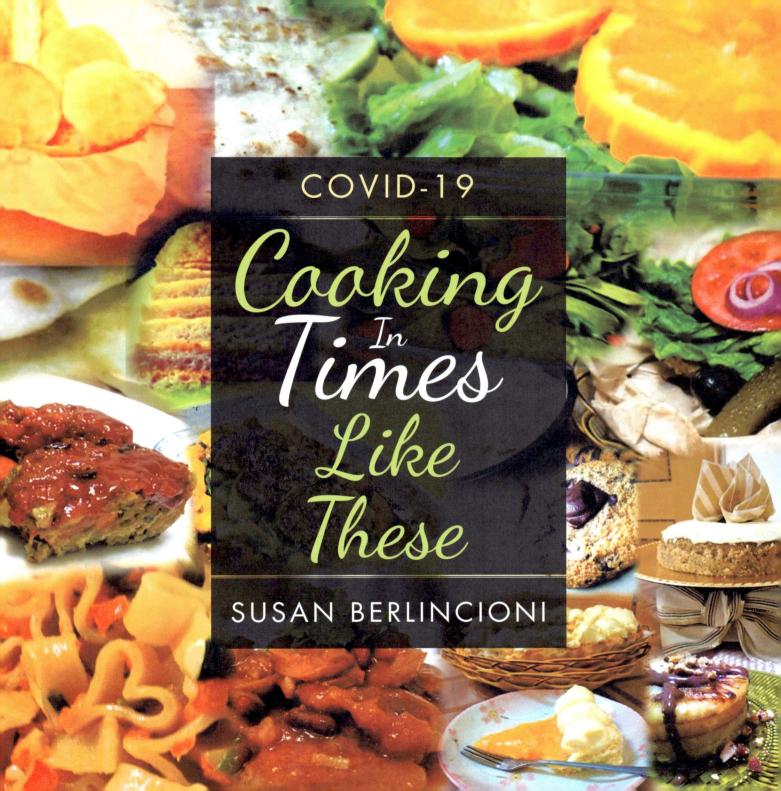

COVID-19

Cooking
In
Times
Like
These

SUSAN BERLINCIONI

Balboa Press books may be ordered through booksellers or by contacting:

A Division of Hay House
1663 Liberty Drive
Bloomington, IN 47403
www.balboapress.com
844-682-1282

ISBN: 978-1-9822-4809-3 (sc)
ISBN: 978-1-9822-4810-9 (e)

Library of Congress Control Number: 2020910131

Print information available on the last page.

Balboa Press rev. date: 12/07/2020

BALBOA.PRESS

Cooking In Times Like These

Stand in Unity

Take heart knowing that 100% of the net profits received from the sale of this cookbook from Balboa Press will be donated to feed those in need.

How you can help.

1) Make a gift to mail out to someone in quarantine. Show them they are in your thoughts during such a testing time.

2) Purchase this cookbook to cook for someone in need. Share the love for one another.

3) Make a direct donation through our website in order to feed those in need at *http://www.liveoutyourlight.com*

To order additional copies of this cookbook, please visit us at *http://www.liveoutyourlight.com*

Dedication

Special thanks to all my life teachers who let me understand~
that everyone can do something to make someone else's life better.

And that everyone included me.

Contents

1   We Are All in This Together 1

2   How Can We Get Through This? 3

3   Cooking in These Times 7

4   Food Shopping, Food Preparation, and Food Storing in These Times 9

5   Recipes 14

6   Recipe Suitability Guide 61

Disclaimer

Nothing in this book is intended to be read, taken, or experimented with as a medical form of treatment. This information is for the sole purpose of a suggestion of a lifestyle. The information provided is offered as a preventive care option. It is not in any way to replace medical advice given by a medical doctor. Furthermore, one should consult with their family physician before starting any type of new lifestyle change regardless whether it be food, nutrition, or otherwise.

This book does not provide medical advice. It is intended for informational purposes only. It is not a substitute for professional medical advice, diagnosis or treatment. Never ignore professional medical advice in seeking treatment because of something you have read. If you think you may have a medical emergency, immediately call your doctor or dial 911.

Acknowledgements

Firstly, I need to thank Louise Hay for her contribution to a greater humanity. Her conviction that we can all grow to into a greater version of ourselves, by loving ourselves and others. That homework has really hit home for me. I would like to thank all of the patient, kind, and knowledgeable people at Balboa Press. As they are all interwoven in the pages of this book. Their insight, suggestions and editing were the "cherry on top of the cake".

Thanks to our team of tech experts. Their valued input has helped us to let people find hope in their kitchen~ by easily finding us on the world wide web. And undoubtedly this work would not have been possible without Ferretti. His positive feedback of each recipe and food photography abilities are what made this book become three-dimensional.

Chapter One
We Are All in This Together

At the time of this writing... I was born and raised a USA girl. I am in love with a great burger and fries. And I surely cannot live without a Chicago style deep dish pizza now and again. I grew up watching The Food Network channel as my go-to. When I was about eight months pregnant, I had that channel on 24/7. I would talk to my womb and tell my baby about all the delicious foods I was going to make for him after he was born. And so I did.

After my son was born, my husband and I had to make some serious decisions about our son's schooling, our careers, and our lives. Fast forward many years we are now working and living in Asia. In early January of 2020, the government closed all the schools and asked everyone to stay home and stay put. Airlines were discouraged, and citizens were homebound—some in self-quarantine and some in hospitals. The news was depressing. How could we cope? And how do we have hope? How can we thrive in a situation like this?

These were the questions I asked myself. I asked my own self. What can I do to help others in need? How can I reach people living by themselves? How can I reach people who must live in quarantine and isolation? Soon the answer hit me in the head. A voice said do what you do best. Cook for them! What? How can I reach them? And cook for who? Cook for all the nations and all the ethnics and all the ages. Cook and be merry again! And so I did.

This is my contribution to humanity. Please enjoy it!

Chapter 2
How Can We Get Through This?

At this point in history, we can all agree that everyone's life has been altered or changed in some way. This is a global situation. We all have to think, act, and yes implement, our lives differently from this day forward. There are pros and cons to this situation. So, let's dive into the pros straight away.

We all have a lot of free time indoors. (Yes, it is a bit hard at first.) After talking with myself, the optimistic sunshine came through again. How many times have you watched a DYI on YouTube and muttered to yourself "Oh I'd love to try that but I don't have the time". We've all said it time and time again. Well, now, we have time. So, let's do it!

Let's consider, that this is a special time in history. And that it will not last forever. The situation will finish at some point, and we will all get back to a familiar routine. While being indoors, our top priority is to stay safe and virus free as possible.

The suggestions in this book are offered by an everyday mom who has loved cooking all her life. And wanted to share it with others. I am not a medical professional. And I am not medically advising anyone. What I am sharing is how I have kept many past viruses away. Again, and again every cold season by using food and herbs. If you are on a special diet or taking certain medicines, please consult with your doctor before making any dietary changes.

The symptoms of this virus have been stated so far as, cough, sore throat, loss of taste, loss of smell, heavy fatigue, depression, and few have vomiting. So, let's dive into each category, shall we?

Cough and Sore Throat

By far my family uses natural *honey* for passing cold season every year. We literally have not needed cough medicine or antibiotics in 10 years. Why? Because we have adapted to real honey drinks daily and replaced honey for fructose sugar in our everyday diet. Next there is fresh *ginger*. It is wonderful to have a cup of ginger tea. As well as using ginger regularly in your meal preparation. If you do not already use ginger, I can assure you, you will be pleasantly surprised. If you give it a try.

Thyme has both culinary and medicinal uses for centuries as a remedy for cough and even bronchitis.

Pineapple has an anti-inflammatory property called *bromelain*. Which means it can breakdown mucus, and remove it from the body. Pineapple is also high in vitamin C. Immune boosting foods which contain vitamin C, like fresh lemons, oranges, pineapple and kiwi are quite helpful.

Other sources of vitamin C are listed below. These are foods that we have regularly eaten daily, which is why our immune system has been strong over the years—and not needing any pharmaceutical drugs for ten years now.

So, with this virus around, we are doubling up on our nutritional intake, in an effort to keep this virus far away.

Most Common & Easily Purchased Vitamin C Food List

Chili Peppers
Sweet Yellow Peppers
Thyme
Parsley
Spinach mustard variety
Kale
Broccoli
Lemons
Oranges
Strawberries

We will be using these ingredients as part of a balanced diet and lifestyle in order to stay safe and fight off this virus. As far as keeping our body well hydrated, drinking water is ideal. But if you have a family like mine, who are more meat eaters than water drinkers then a great way around that is to serve meals on beds of hydrating vegetables. Below is a list of the most common and easily purchased hydrating fruits & vegetables.

Most Common Easily Purchased Hydrating Fruits & Vegetables List

Lettuce
Zucchini
Tomato
Celery
Radish
Spinach
Cucumber
Watermelon
Strawberries

And finally, we opted for foods on our Super Food List. We are specifically using the ones that are most common and most easily purchased. The edited list is as follows.

Most Common Easily Purchased Super Foods List

Berries
Fish
Leafy Greens
Nuts
Olive Oil
Whole Grains
Yogurt
Cruciferous Vegetables
Legumes
Tomatoes

Loss of Taste and Smell

To compensate for the loss of taste and smell, we have used fresh herbs whenever possible. Since the start of this virus, we have started our own indoor boxed herb garden again. We will have tutorial videos available for you to start your own garden. (Since you have the time.)

Fatigue

This one can attack us throughout our lifetime. I personally had a medical situation in the past, which caused me a great deal of fatigue. To combat this, I had to make a great effort to remake the recipes within 15 to 20 minutes of cooking time. Anyone going through fatigue symptoms, may want to consider using the auto shut off timer button on their oven.

Story

I remember many times putting things in the oven to bake and unknowingly falling asleep in the middle of the day. This was due to my fatigue symptoms. So, an auto shut off button would be ideal if at all possible.

Vomiting

Many recipes here can be put on dry toast, dry rice cakes, or topped over cooked plain rice or pasta. These help to settle the stomach. Also eating just, a bit in the beginning. If your condition allows it. You may gradually increase your portions as your health improves.

Depression

When I had depression, the first thing that came to my mind was comfort food. Eating comfort food can help us emotionally feel better. For that reason, I also have listed crowd-pleaser comfort food recipes, which I have readapted to eat during this virus.

There we have it! We are fully armored with immune-building foods, hydrating foods, and superfoods. Recipes that will help aid in healing your body, and will comfort your soul.

Chapter 3
Cooking in These Times

———◆━◆━◆———

Things to consider in order to get through this time with flying colors...

We all as humans resist change. That's how we are wired. So, going forward, you will see recipes prepared in perhaps ways you may never expect. I certainly never expected it in my past 30 years of cooking. Well, here we are. All of us globally fighting an enemy we cannot even see. So please, please, stay with me. And let's cook together!

All recipes will be four servings unless specified differently. The recipes can all be doubled accordingly. Or cut in half if needed. The recipes can be frozen without compromising taste. Which is an aid for days when fatigue or depression strike.

The main theme right now is nutrition and comfort foods. We need to be comforted. Whether you're home alone or not. Whether or not you're in quarantine, we really need to get happy. Each recipe lists whether it's better suited for Western-style, Asian style, keto diet, vegan, crowd-pleaser, or kid-friendly. Please hear me when I say with LOVE if you are home and alone and in quarantine. Perhaps now is not the ideal time to be worrying and have stress about calories intake levels of losing weight. You need to feed your body and soul with the rich nutrient foods to increase your immune system. Again, if you have any concerns before trying the recipes, you may place a telephone call to your doctor's office. The goal here is to increase the body's natural healing power by using foods as one of the items in your artillery, which brings me to a story of many years ago.

Story

I had a friend who struggled with alcoholism. He was also a smoker. And he was trying to gain weight. He told me he wanted to start attending AAA classes. But he didn't have transportation. So, I agreed to bring him to start off. I will never forget the speaker on the first night. She said something that stayed with me forever. It went something like this... If you're here to quit drinking, that's great. So, let's get into it. Now, if you want to stop drinking, stop smoking cigarettes, and stop drugs... well, we have to talk. Start with ~stop drinking only~. After you conquer the drinking issue, you can later move on to stopping the cigarettes, and so on. If you insist on stopping everything at once, you are setting yourself up for failure. Please don't waste your time like that.

Chapter 4
Food Shopping, Food Preparation, and Food Storing in These Times

---

People have often been surveyed about what they felt was the biggest drawback of cooking at home. Results showed that going to the market to buy the ingredients was the most taxing after a long day at work. (And the long lines were a big deterrent.) Given that factor and the food availability, there is a need to consider either planning out a few weeks of the menu at a time or cooking with items that can be easily delivered to your doorstep. This may seem absurd to you. As my Italian relative said once, "How will I know what I feel like eating weeks in advance!!!" She is the same relative who eats cold cut sandwiches for dinner most nights of the week. She says, "there was nothing in the house to cook with, so I just made a sandwich". By buying your ingredients a week or two in advance, you are giving yourself much more options. Can you imagine someone ordering a pizza for dinner, and the chef saying, "Oh let me run to the market now to buy the tomatoes and cheese". Of course not!

There is another way of looking at it. For example, what could you make with a can of tomatoes and some cheese? It might surprise you!

1. Pizza
2. Quesadillas
3. Baked tomatoes and cheese
4. Sliced tomato and mozzarella cheese on the grill
5. Cheesy tomato beef skillet
6. Tomato soup topped with cheese
7. Tomato and cheese pasta
8. Grilled cheese with tomato toasts
9. Lasagna
10. Eggplant parmesan
11. Tomato, cheese, and basil dip

12. Beans baked in tomatoes and cheese
13. Chicken baked in tomatoes and cheese
14. Greek style quiche
15. Mediterranean tart
16. Mexican tomato and cheese salsa
17. Chicken and cheese entermodus
18. Portuguese eggs baked in tomatoes and cheese
19. Porto's Francesinha sandwich
20. Baked Cod with herbed cheese and tomato

The choice is really up to you. The comment I explained to my relative was by buying some ingredients in advance, you give yourself *more* options. Like in the example above I have 20 choices about what to do with my can of tomato and cheese. If I wait to the last minute, I end up with the same boring sandwich. Or said in another way, I end up with no choice at all.

Food Ingredients

Many towns and cities have reported a decline in fresh items at the moment. I personally had to go to three different shops to buy my daily bread. And they were all sold out and waiting for delivery. After hearing that I went home and started making my own bread again. And why not? I surely have the time! Factoring that some people are home alone and in quarantine changes how we shop for food. The safest way to get food is to buy it online nowadays and have it delivered. Few companies will ship or deliver fresh, raw meats, dairy, and certain types of vegetables or fruits. So, we need to get creative in the kitchen!

You will notice that each recipe will use either vacuum packed or tinned meats, fish, canned fruits, and vegetables. And in some cases, we even have a cream that can keep without refrigeration. Please check the resource guide to buy this item online if they are not easily available where you live. See how you can get these items delivered to your door at https://liveoutyourlight.com

· ·

If you can buy fresh meats, fish, vegetables, and cheese you may consider putting them in the freezer. Yes, it does change the integrity a bit. This is considerable during this virus and a shortage of items time. Being of European blood everything goes well with some cheese. In France as well as Italy there are an average of 2,000 plus recorded varieties of cheese. Can you imagine that? How wonderful for cheese lovers. When I was a little girl my mother used to make homemade cheese...

Story

I was overjoyed when I saw Jamie Oliver on his show saying that it's OK to freeze cheese in a pinch. Since then I freeze almost all my cheeses if needed. The dry varieties bought vacuum-packed are quick to put into the freezer. I take my tubes of cream cheese and triple wrap them in foil and zip-lock them in a freezer bag. When we have a blizzard weekend, my friends come over for homemade brownies with cream cheese. Delicious!

These recipes are all freezable. Unless stated otherwise. After you finish cooking you can put it in a zip-lock freezer bag and store it. Put it immediately in the refrigerator to cool down if you like. Then once it stops steaming press the air out of the bag, lock it, and lay it flat in your freezer. Never leave food to cool down on the counter as you can incur the risk of food poisoning.

<u>Time and Space</u>

I have heard from some of my friends that their entire family has been homebound for a month now. One of my friends said she's never been home with the entire family for more than one day! That takes some adjusting too, especially in the kitchen. In most average homes there is only one kitchen. If you're the cook you may not have the luxury of having the kitchen all to yourself. Instead, you may perhaps feel like you're in Grand Central station.

Another factor is that there may be multiple people needing to cook something. So, you may or may not be able to linger around in the kitchen. Which is another reason why these recipes were designed to be ready within 20 minutes.

Given the fact that in some households people eat at different times. Grandmother eats at one time, parents eat at another time, kids eat late, and the baby eats all the time! So, these recipes were created so that even children, aged seven and above, could easily or by watching our online tutorials make these recipes for the other members of the family. With adult supervision.

Budget Friendly Recipes

All recipes have been designed with nutrition as well as cost in mind. Noting that we all really do not know how long this will last. And how long some of us are not working. Others not working because they were infected, and need to be home to recover.

Following Government Safety Requests

At this time there have been reports from the Health Authorities stating that it is advised to wash all foods and food containers before putting them into the refrigerator. Please see the viral post which discussed it here at https://www.healthline.com/health-news/worried-about-contaminated-groceries-how-to-be-safe. This will add more time in the kitchen. But certainly, a worthwhile step in adding to our artillery of resources in the fight against the unknown enemy.

♥

So, take my heart and take my hand. Come and cook with me.
Put to rest the uncertainties that lie ahead of you and me.
We don't need much but it sure will taste like a lot!

♥

Love and peace to all the world.

♥

There is something magical about making your own bread. For a super treat pop bread in the oven before having breakfast. The aroma of fresh baked bread will fill the air. And transform your start.

Daily Bread

- ◆ 500g all-purpose flour
- ◆ 1 oz butter or margarine
- ◆ 1 ¼ tsp salt
- ◆ 1 ½ tsp fast action yeast
- ◆ 10 fl oz warm water

In a large bowl, mix together flour and salt, rub in the butter or margarine. Then stir in the yeast. Slowly add in the water to make a soft dough with your hands.

Knead the dough for about 5 minutes in an electric food mixer, or knead by hand for about 10 minutes on a floured work surface. Shape the dough and then place it in a greased baking pan or dish. To make individual buns divide the dough into 6 balls. Flatten the dough in a 3.5-inch diameter circle about ⅜ thick. Cover with a clean damp tea towel, and let rise until about double in size. About 1 ½ hours.

For one single loaf, uncover and bake in a preheated oven of 450F/230C/ for about 30 to 35 minutes. For the individual buns uncover and bake in a preheated oven of 350F/180C for 12 minutes. Remove from the oven to see if done. If needed, turn the pan around in the oven and bake a few minutes more.

Take the bread(s) out of the baking pan and let it cool on a rack.

Nutritional Content Information
- ‣ Servings 10
- ‣ Calories 204
- ‣ Protein 22
- ‣ Carbs 156
- ‣ Fat 25

Come and cook this recipe along with us at http://www.liveoutyourlight.com

This is a fantastic way to change a boring sandwich into an awesome event. Try it and you will see.

Flat Bread

- ◆ 1 cup all-purpose flour or gluten-free flour
- ◆ 2 tsp baking powder
- ◆ 1 cup full fat natural plain yogurt
  (or Greek yogurt)
- ◆ ¼ cup butter melted or oil

In a large bowl, combine the flour and baking powder. Then gently add in the yogurt bit by bit. You may need less than a cup. Which is ok. Mix well. Then use your hands to bring the dough together gently.

Your dough has now shaped into a nice ball. Flour your work surface and cut your dough into 6 even pieces. Roll out each mini ball as evenly as possible.

Heat a nonstick skillet over medium heat and brush one side of the bread. Place the brushed side down into the pan. Allow cooking about 2-3 minutes per side. Noting that the bread will bubble up. Turn bread over and watch it bubble up quickly. Remove from pan. Repeat until all the bread has been cooked.

Nutritional Content Information
- ➤ Servings 6
- ➤ Calories 101
- ➤ Protein 14
- ➤ Carbs 73
- ➤ Fat 13

Come and cook this recipe along with us at http://www.liveoutyourlight.com

This is by far the best and quickest BBQ sauce. It's great for outdoor and indoor grilling.

BBQ Sauce

- ◆ 14-ounce diced tomatoes, drained
- ◆ 1 can/6-ounce tomato paste
- ◆ ½ cup brown sugar, or syrup of molasses
- ◆ 3 Tbsp apple cider vinegar
- ◆ salt, pepper, garlic powder, chili powder, to taste

Put all the ingredients into a blender and whiz. Start adding your seasoning bit by bit until you reach the desired flavor you like. Refrigerate for up to three days or freeze in a freezer zip-lock bag for up to three months.

Nutritional Content Information
- ➤ Servings 6
- ➤ Calories 81
- ➤ Protein 6
- ➤ Carbs 72
- ➤ Fat 2

Come and cook this recipe along with us at http://www.liveoutyourlight.com

This is a very versatile sauce that can be made spicy or just deliciously sweet.

Sweet Thai (Chile) Sauce

- ◆ 1 cup distilled white vinegar
- ◆ ⅓ cup sugar
- ◆ 1 Thai chili or other if desired
- ◆ 2 cloves garlic, minced
- ◆ ¾ cup plus 2 Tbsp water, divided
- ◆ 2 Tbsp cornstarch

Combine the first four ingredients with ¾ cup of water. Microwave for about 2 minutes in order to melt the sugar. Alternatively, stir in a small sauce pan over low-medium heat. Be careful as it will be very hot and bubbling. Mix the cornstarch with the remaining water. Add the cornstarch mixture to the other cooled mixture. Refrigerate for up to three days or freeze in freezer zip-lock bags for up to three months.

Nutritional Content Information
- ‣ Servings 10
- ‣ Calories 90
- ‣ Protein 0
- ‣ Carbs 89
- ‣ Fat 0

Come and cook this recipe along with us at http://www.liveoutyourlight.com

This is a shocking sauce because your guests will exclaim, "So this is what homemade buffalo sauce tastes like."

Buffalo Sauce

- ♦ ½ cup melted butter or margarine
- ♦ ¼-½ cup hot sauce, fresh or bottled
- ♦ 2 Tbsp distilled white vinegar
- ♦ 2 tsp Worcestershire sauce

In a bowl, whisk together all ingredients until well blended. Store in an airtight container in the fridge for up to three days. Shake well each time before using.

Nutritional Content Information
- ➤ Servings 10
- ➤ Calories 85
- ➤ Protein 0
- ➤ Carbs 3
- ➤ Fat 81

Come and cook this recipe along with us at http://www.liveoutyourlight.com

Often, I will serve this to my vegan friends with the homemade flat bread listed on page 15.
It's always a hit!

Enchilada Sauce

- ◆ ¼ cup olive oil
- ◆ ¼ cup all-purpose flour
- ◆ 3 Tbsp chili powder
- ◆ 1 cup both or spring water
- ◆ 1 can/28-ounce crushed tomatoes
- ◆ 1 Tbsp packed brown sugar
- ◆ Spice mix of 1 tsp each of dried oregano, cumin, garlic powder, onion, salt to taste

Gently heat olive oil in sauce pan and add flour. Whisk the sauce in the pan. Slowly add each of the remaining ingredients bit by bit. Taste carefully. And adjust the seasoning to your liking.

This recipe makes about four cups of sauce. Refrigerate for up to three days or freeze in freezer zip-lock bags for up to three months.

Nutritional Content Information
- ➤ Servings 6
- ➤ Calories 88
- ➤ Protein 6
- ➤ Carbs 34
- ➤ Fat 47

Come and cook this recipe along with us at http://www.liveoutyourlight.com

This sauce goes such a long way in flavor. This can be a great sheet-pan style served with sweet and white potatoes and choice of meats.

Jerk Seasoning Mix

- ¼ cup onion powder
- 2 Tbsp salt
- 2 Tbsp thyme
- 2 tsp ground allspice
- 1 Tbsp cinnamon
- 1 tsp cayenne pepper

Mix all the spices in a bowl. Mix it well. Then put it in an airtight container. It will store for months if sealed properly. This recipe will yield approximately 2 cups.

Nutritional Content Information
- ‣ Servings 16
- ‣ Calories 27
- ‣ Protein 1g
- ‣ Carbs 6g
- ‣ Fat 0g

If you ever felt squeamish about buying spices just for a teaspoon needed... then making your own spice mixes will rectify that. And using this Adobe mix will surely be worth your while.

Adobe Seasoning Mix

- ◆ ⅓ cup garlic powder
- ◆ ⅓ cup salt
- ◆ ¼ cup each of oregano, turmeric, onion powder
- ◆ 3 Tbsp pepper
- ◆ 2 tsp paprika
- ◆ 1 Tbsp chili powder
- ◆ 1 teaspoon ground cumin seeds, optional

Add all ingredients in an airtight container. Shake well. Store for months in an airtight container. This recipe will yield approximately 2 cups.

Nutritional Content Information
- ‣ Servings 10
- ‣ Calories 56
- ‣ Protein 2g
- ‣ Carbs 13g
- ‣ Fat 1g

I will keep this recipe on hand, to serve to my vegan friends. When they surprisingly stop by. They love it!

Quesadillas

- ◆ 8 flour tortillas
- ◆ ¾ cup of shredded Monterrey Jack cheese or Pepper Jack cheese
- ◆ 4 scallions thinly sliced
- ◆ ¼ cup chopped fresh cilantro
- ◆ ½ cup mild or hot prepared salsa

Take one tortilla wrap at a time. Layer it with some cheese, scallions, and cilantro. Generously then spread some salsa over the mixture. Top the wrap with another tortilla wrap. Seal the ends. At this point, you may either heat them gently in an oven for about 5 minutes to warm through and let the cheese melt. Or you may heat them gently in a nonstick skillet. Whichever you prefer, they are delicious.

Nutritional Content Information
- ‣ Servings 8
- ‣ Calories 520
- ‣ Protein 18g
- ‣ Carbs 100g
- ‣ Fat 6g

Come and cook this recipe along with us at http://www.liveoutyourlight.com

I always disliked peanut sauce until I made this one. It can change your mind.

Peanut Sauce

- ♦ 6 quarter-sized slices of fresh ginger, peeled
- ♦ 3 Tbsp plus 2 Tbsp soy sauce with garlic
- ♦ 1 Tbsp dark sesame seed oil
- ♦ ⅓ cup creamy peanut butter
- ♦ ¼ cup spring water or broth
- ♦ ¼ teaspoon red pepper flakes, optional

In a food processor combine the ginger and mince. Add the 3 Tbsp soy sauce and sesame oil and pulse again. Now you may add your choice of meat to this marinade and put it in the refrigerator to marinate as long as possible. Meanwhile, prepare the rest of the sauce. In a small bowl, combine the peanut butter, the water or broth, and the remaining 2 tablespoons of soy sauce. Add in the red pepper flakes if you are using them. After grilling the meats pour the peanut sauce over the meat and serve on a platter. This sauce must be used within three days while kept in the fridge.

Nutritional Content Information
- ‣ Servings 6
- ‣ Calories 119
- ‣ Protein 4g
- ‣ Carbs 6g
- ‣ Fat 9g

Come and cook this recipe along with us at http://www.liveoutyourlight.com

The ultimate in comfort food. This recipe is worth its' weight in gold. I always make an extra pan to put in the freezer. As you will taste why.

15-Minute Lasagna x 3

To make Basic 15-Minute Red Tomato Sauce proceed as follows

- ◆ 2 Tbsp olive oil
- ◆ 6 cloves of fresh garlic minced
- ◆ 1 small white onion, finely chopped
- ◆ half of a can or about 190 grams tomato paste
- ◆ spring water, half of tomato paste can x3
- ◆ ¼ cup red wine, optional

To make simple tomato sauce in 15 minutes proceed as follows. Put the olive oil in a medium-size sauté pan. Let the oil heat a bit. Then add onion and sauté for about 6 minutes. Add the garlic and sauté about two minutes more. Add in the tomato paste and the water. Keep stirring until the sauce thickens a bit. Add in the red wine if you are using it. Stir through again and season with salt and pepper.

To make a 15-Minute Lasagna x3 proceed as follows

- 1 batch tomato sauce listed above
- 1 bunch spinach, fresh or frozen, washed/defrosted & well drained
- 1-2 cups cooked seasoned ground meat, if desired
- 2 cups of your favorite shredded melting cheese
- ¼ cup Parmesan Reggiano cheese
- Lasagna sheets no boil

Come and cook this recipe along with us at http://www.liveoutyourlight.com

Take a rectangular pan and put a few drops of olive oil in the bottom. Then add a very small layer of tomato sauce. Then add the lasagna sheets to cover the bottom of the pan. Start layer with tomato sauce, then meat, if using, then spinach, if using, then cheeses. Repeat layers ending with the cheese. Loosely cover your lasagna with foil to avoid it from browning too quickly.

At this point, you may triple wrap your lasagna and put it in a freezer zip-lock bag. It can be stored in the freezer for near to three months.

Alternatively, place your lasagna in a preheated oven of 350F/180C to let the flavors marry for about 10 minutes or so. Then remove the top foil from your pan and let the cheese brown for no more than five minutes.

Buon Appetito.

....

Red Tomato Sauce only
- ➤ Nutritional Content Information
- ➤ Servings 6
- ➤ Calories 75
- ➤ Protein 0g
- ➤ Carbs 5g
- ➤ Fat 0g

15-Minute Lasagna completed
- ➤ Nutritional Content Information
- ➤ Servings 6
- ➤ Calories 302
- ➤ Protein 17g
- ➤ Carbs 9g
- ➤ Fat 23g

This is a great kids' recipe. Hide healthy vegetables under a fruit salsa sauce with fried plantains.

Island Styled Chicken and Rice with Salsa

- ¾ cup onion, chopped
- ½ cup bell pepper or chili pepper minced
- 1 tsp fresh thyme, minced or half a tsp of dried thyme
- 2 cloves of garlic, minced
- 2 boneless chicken breasts, about 8 ounces, skins removed

- ¾ tsp salt and pepper to taste
- 1-2 Tbsp olive oil
- 8-ounce diced tomatoes, well-drained
- 1 Serrano chili, optional

Combine the first six ingredients in a bowl. Place the chicken into the bowl of marinade and toss to coat. Refrigerate while preparing the rest of the recipe. Meanwhile, heat the oil in a large nonstick skillet or sauté pan until hot. Remove chicken from marinade, and sauté in hot oil for about one minute or so per side. You will see that the chicken has taken on a browned color. Discard the marinade. Or, if you wish, add the marinade into the pan. Add a bit of salt, the tomatoes, and the chili, if using. Bring this mixture to a boil. Cover and reduce the heat to similar 5 to 6 minutes or so. Serve this dish with Island Salsa, cooked plantains, and rice if you wish. The recipe for the salsa is listed below.

Nutritional Content Information
- Servings 4
- Calories 208
- Protein 13g
- Carbs 9g
- Fat 6g

Come and cook this recipe along with us at http://www.liveoutyourlight.com

Island Salsa

- ¼ cup brown sugar
- a few drops or up to 3 Tbsp of white rum
- 2 Tbsp fresh lime juice
- 4 cups fresh pineapple cubes
- one-star fruit (Carambola) thinly sliced

....

In a small pan gently warm the sugar and white rum. Over very low heat just to melt the sugar. Remove it from the heat and toss in a bowl with the other ingredients. Chill until ready to serve cold.

....

Nutritional Content Information
- Servings 4
- Calories 130
- Protein 1g
- Carbs 27g
- Fat 0g

Come and cook this recipe along with us at http://www.liveoutyourlight.com

Sautéed Plantains

- ◆ 1 Tbsp of cooking oil
- ◆ 2 small Plantain bananas, peeled and sliced lengthwise

....

Heat the oil in a nonstick pan. When the oil is hot add the plantains slowly into the pan. Being very careful, fry them in oil for about 1 ½ minutes per side. They will take on a browned color. Remove them from the oil and place them on paper towels. Serve immediately. This recipe requires adult supervision at all times.

....

Nutritional Content Information
- ➤ Servings 4
- ➤ Calories 120
- ➤ Protein 1g
- ➤ Carbs 32g
- ➤ Fat 0g

Whether you're a die-core chili fan or not read on. This is a must to try. And don't forget plenty of cornbread!

Hot or Spicy Chorizo Chili

- 4 Tbsp olive oil
- 14-ounce tomatoes, well- drained
- Chipotle chilies in Adobo sauce, optional
- 1 pd vacuum packed, spicy chorizo sausage, thinly sliced
- one very large white onion, thinly sliced
- 2 Tbsp garlic, minced
- ¾ cup of chicken broth
- 6-ounce lemon-lime carbonated soda
- ¼ cup dry red wine or broth
- 30-ounce beans, red or black
- 1-ounce unsweetened dark chocolate, well chopped
- salt to taste
- ⅛ cup fresh lime or lemon juice
- ⅛ cup chopped fresh cilantro
- sour cream, if desired

In a food processor, whiz tomatoes and chili's if using. Set aside.

Then heat a big pan or pot about 5 quarts with the oil. Add in one at a time the chorizo and onions. Sauté for about 7 minutes. Then add the garlic and salt to taste, if desired. Cook a few minutes more. Stir in the tomatoes, broth, carbonated beverage, wine, beans, and chocolate. Heat to boiling, reduce heat, and simmer to desired consistency. Season with salt, to taste.

When serving add the lime juice and garnish with cilantro and sour cream if desired.

Nutritional Content Information
- Servings 4
- Calories 229
- Protein 12g
- Carbs 44g
- Fat 3g

Come and cook this recipe along with us at http://www.liveoutyourlight.com

This is a hands down winner in every category. This can be marinated in meats, vegetables, or both. With grand success!

Honey Delight Sauce

- ◆ 2 tsp fresh garlic, minced
- ◆ 1 Tbsp ginger, finally grated
- ◆ 1 Tbsp bottled oyster or fish sauce
- ◆ 1 Tbsp soy sauce, low sodium
- ◆ ¼ cup honey
- ◆ two fillets of pork or breast meat
- ◆ 1 Tbsp peanut oil* for frying
- ◆ 2 green onions, finely sliced for garnish

In a zip-lock bag, combine the first five ingredients. Mix well. Add the meat. Seal the bag and refrigerate until ready to use. Meanwhile, add the peanut oil (*you may substitute for cooking oil, if you do not like the peanuts, or if you are allergic to nuts) into a nonstick pan. Remove the meat from the bag. And place the meat in the pan. Cook the meat a few minutes for each side. The meat will take on a beautiful dark caramel look as it cooks. Serve with plain white rice and sprinkled with green onions if you like.

Nutritional Content Information
- ➤ Servings 4
- ➤ Calories 96
- ➤ Protein 3g
- ➤ Carbs 19g
- ➤ Fat 1g

Come and cook this recipe along with us at http://www.liveoutyourlight.com

This recipe came in as a last-minute attempt to get dinner on the table within twenty minutes. It's still on our table thirty years later.

Thyme Marinade

- ◆ 1 ½ cups of thyme vinegar, store-bought or homemade
- ◆ half cup of spring water
- ◆ 2 Tbsp garlic, minced
- ◆ ¼ tsp red pepper chili flakes
- ◆ ½ tsp onion salt
- ◆ ¼ tsp ground black pepper

....

Combine all the ingredients in a zip-lock bag. Mix well. Add your favorite meat and or vegetables. Refrigerate overnight for best flavor. When desired, remove contents from marinade. Discard marinade. And grill in a BBQ or skillet.

....

Nutritional Content Information
- ➤ Servings 4
- ➤ Calories 26
- ➤ Protein 0
- ➤ Carbs 2
- ➤ Fat 0

Come and cook this recipe along with us at http://www.liveoutyourlight.com

This is a wonderful meal, if ever there was one. Made in minutes, to free you to enjoy with your guests.

Pesto with Sun Dried Tomatoes

- ♦ ½ cup sun-dried tomatoes
- ♦ ½ cup black olives, chopped
- ♦ 6-ounce jar of artichoke hearts with natural liquid, chopped
- ♦ 2 Tbsp fresh parsley, minced
- ♦ 4 Tbsp olive oil
- ♦ salt and pepper to taste

- ♦ 1 cup Gruyère cheese, cut into tiny cubes

Add the first 6 ingredients to a zip-lock bag. Mix well. Allow to marinade in the fridge as long as possible to let the flavors marry. This recipe may be enjoyed over grilled meats or cooked pasta. For the meats, pour over cooked marinade meats. Then sprinkle with the cheese. For pasta, take half a pound of hot cooked pasta and toss it with the Gruyère cheese. Then add in the marinated pesto. Serve immediately.

Nutritional Content Information
- ➤ Servings 4
- ➤ Calories 312
- ➤ Protein 12
- ➤ Carbs 9
- ➤ Fat 26

Come and cook this recipe along with us at http://www.liveoutyourlight.com

This is such a healthy dish that can be served equally as well with cooked pasta, rice, or a side dish.

Lemon Braised Broccoli Rabé

- ♦ one large bunch of broccoli Rabé or regular broccoli cut into edible pieces
- ♦ 2 Tbsp olive oil
- ♦ 3 garlic cloves, minced
- ♦ 2 lemons, rind peeled into thin strips

Blanch broccoli rabé in boiling water for 1 to 2 minutes, depending on the thickness of the stems. Rinse in cold water and put aside. Then using a large nonstick skillet or sauté pan to heat the olive oil over medium heat. Add in the garlic and stir gently about a minute or two. Stir in the broccoli rabé and add the salt and pepper. Squeeze the juice of one lemon into the sauce. Remove from heat. Mix the broccoli with the garlic mixture. Toss with lemon rind strips. At this point you may serve this dish as a side dish. As well you may enjoy to serve this with half a pound of cooked shaped pasta. In that instance, toss a pound of cooked shaped pasta with half a cup of Parmesan Reggiano cheese. Then add the broccoli mixture and top with the lemon rind strips.

Nutritional Content Information
- ‣ Servings 4
- ‣ Calories 113
- ‣ Protein 4
- ‣ Carbs 12
- ‣ Fat 7

Come and cook this recipe along with us at http://www.liveoutyourlight.com

This is an Italian version of eating peanut butter from the jar! It goes well with everything like sandwiches, crackers, bagels, and picnics.

Ricotta and Bean Paté

- ◆ 2 cloves garlic, peeled
- ◆ 14-ounce can beans, borlotti, navy, or butter well drained and rinsed
- ◆ ¾ cup ricotta cheese or cream cheese
- ◆ 4 Tbsp melted butter
- ◆ ½ cup fresh lemon juice
- ◆ 2 Tbsp fresh parsley
- ◆ 1 Tbsp fresh thyme or 1 tsp dried thyme

In a food processor, start adding in each ingredient one by one. Whiz for a few seconds for each item added. A delicious creamy paté will naturally form.

This paté may be stored in a glass serving dish with a cover in the fridge for about a week. Serve it with breads, rice crackers, quick sandwiches, and even as a party dip.

Nutritional Content Information
- ➤ Servings 8
- ➤ Calories 96
- ➤ Protein 3
- ➤ Carbs 2
- ➤ Fat 9

Come and cook this recipe along with us at http://www.liveoutyourlight.com

This is a definite five-star crowd pleaser. Make additional sauce to cook with your choice of vegetables. And you will be the talk of the town.

Mini Meat Loaves

- ◆ 1 Tbsp olive oil
- ◆ 1 sweet red bell pepper, cored and chopped fine
- ◆ 3 green onions, thinly sliced
- ◆ 2 cloves of garlic, well minced
- ◆ 1 Tbsp fresh thyme or ¼ tsp dried thyme

- ◆ 1 ½ pounds of ground sirloin beef
- ◆ ¼ pd ground beef 30% fat, minced
- ◆ 2 tsp mustard honey or regular
- ◆ 1 egg, extra large
- ◆ 2 Tbsp ketchup

For the glaze
- ◆ ¼ cup ketchup
- ◆ 2 Tbsp dark brown sugar
- ◆ 1 tsp mustard brown spicy or regular

In a nonstick or sauté pan, heat the olive oil over medium heat. Then add in the red pepper. Sauté for a few minutes until slightly softened. Add in the garlic and sauté for a minute until fragrant. Next, add in the thyme and green onions. Stir together. Remove from heat. Transfer this mixture to a very large bowl. In this large bowl, you will add in the rest of your ingredients, as listed above. Adding in the meats, mustard, the egg, and ketchup. Now massage the loaf using your hands or a wooden spatula. Place the meatloaves in the mini baking tins if using. Bake at 350F/180C in a preheated oven for about 15 minutes.

At this point you may wish to freeze some of the mini loaves. If so, remove them from the baking tins and put them on a tray to cool inside the fridge. When cooled enough to handle, place one mini meatloaf in a zip-lock bag. Press out excess air and seal. Good for up to three months in the freezer. Meanwhile, to make the glaze, use an air tight container. Add in each ingredient and mix well. This mixture can keep well covered in the fridge for a few weeks.

Come and cook this recipe along with us at http://www.liveoutyourlight.com

To finish immediately, remove loaves from oven. Carefully remove them from the tins and place on a baking tray. Brush the tops with the glaze. Return to the oven and allow the glaze to caramelize on the top of the meat loaves. Keep a watchful eye on the loaves and remove them a soon as you see them caramelize. This will happen quickly.

....

Nutritional Content Information
- ▸ Servings 6
- ▸ Calories 830
- ▸ Protein 47
- ▸ Carbs 8
- ▸ Fat 67

My mother would make a fresh pot of this soup for my father, every other day. He is one of the strongest men I have ever known.

Portuguese Kale Soup

- 1 large onion, chopped
- 1 large white potato, diced, any variety
- 1 big bunch of kale, chopped, about 16 ounces
- chorizo sausage, vacuum packed, about 8-ounces, thinly sliced
- 8-ounce white beans, any variety, drained and rinsed
- spring water
- 2 tsp olive oil
- salt to taste

Heat the olive oil in a big pot over medium heat. Add the onion and sauté until softened for about 6 minutes. Add the chorizo and sauté for about 4 minutes more. Turn heat down to the lowest setting. Add in the kale. Then pour in the spring water just to cover the kale. Turn up the heat to boil the soup. Once it starts to bubble, pour in the potatoes, and keep boiling vigorously. So that some of the potatoes will break while cooking. Stir frequently to help the potatoes along. This will take about 5-8 minutes, depending on how small the potatoes were cut. Lastly, stir in the beans and season with salt. Serve immediately.

Nutritional Content Information
- Servings 4
- Calories 463
- Protein 24
- Carbs 41
- Fat 23

Come and cook this recipe along with us at http://www.liveoutyourlight.com

This recipe is dedicated to our dear friend Ed Caincirullo. He would come to the Cranston, RI shop to lunch with us. Being the food Conosur that he is, he would jokingly say, "Oh, we're having Prosciutto di Parma today." To which we would all burst out in laughter. Thank you for the warm memories.

"Mocked Prosciutto di Parma" Sauce for Pasta

- 2 tsp olive oil
- 1 medium white onion, thinly sliced
- 2 springs of green onion, thinly sliced
- 2 cloves garlic, finely chopped
- ⅓ cup white drinking wine
- 6-ounce can ham with cheese luncheon meat
- ½ cup peas, canned or fresh that have been blanched
- 1 cup dairy whipping cream
- salt and pepper to taste
- half pound of pasta

Heat the olive oil in a sauté pan over low to medium heat. Add in the onion and sauté to release its sweetness. After about 7 minutes add the garlic and spring onion. Cook for only a minute more. Push these ingredients to the outer edge of the pan. Add in the luncheon meat and sauté it. Noting that it will stick to the pan. After about 5 minutes pour in the white wine to deglaze the pan. Then mix all ingredients together in the pan. Pour in the cream and the peas and allow it to heat though and slightly thicken. Season with salt and pepper.

To serve, pour the hot sauce over the cooked pasta. Toss gently to coat the pasta evenly. Serve with additional grated Parmesan cheese at the table, if desired.

Nutritional Content Information
- Servings 4
- Calories 279
- Protein 9
- Carbs 51
- Fat 4

Come and cook this recipe along with us at http://www.liveoutyourlight.com

This salad is a tribute to the south of Italy. Where they do such amazing things with citrus. This is a beautiful salad with lovely contrasting colors and shapes. It will make you want to eat. Even if you thought you were not hungry.

An Orange Tree Salad

- ◆ 1 ripe navel orange or blood orange
- ◆ 3 ripe Mandarin oranges
- ◆ 1 key lime, if desired
- ◆ 1 lemon, if desired
- ◆ 1 head of romaine lettuce

....

Triple wash lettuce and hand tear the leaves. Put aside to drip out any excess water. Meanwhile, peel all the citrus fruits. With a very sharp knife, slice the citrus fruits into ¼ inch slices.* (*Adult supervision required at all times.) On your platter, place a layer of lettuce. Then arrange varying slices of citrus to form a colorful polka-dot effect to the eye. Scatter the colors evenly. Repeat the layer again. Ending with the beautiful citrus fruits on top. Keep cold until serving immediately.

....

Nutritional Content Information
- ‣ Servings 4
- ‣ Calories 100
- ‣ Protein 3
- ‣ Carbs 25
- ‣ Fat 1

Come and cook this recipe along with us at http://www.liveoutyourlight.com

A wonderful recipe to have when fresh meat is not on hand. There are many brands of pork in tins. Take your time to select the one which is most suited for you and your loved ones.

Pork Tomato Sauce for Spaghetti Pasta

- ◆ 1 white leek, cleaned and finely sliced
- ◆ 2 cloves garlic, minced
- ◆ 14-ounce can tomatoes, liquid drained
- ◆ ⅓ cup rosé drinking wine
- ◆ 6-ounce can pork cubes
- ◆ 2 tsp olive oil
- ◆ half pound of spaghetti pasta

In a sauté pan heat the olive oil over low to medium heat. Add in the leeks. Sauté gently for about 6 minutes. Then add in the garlic and sauté a minute or so more. Push these ingredients to the outer edge of the pan. Add in the pork cubes and keep sautéing for about 2 minutes. Noting that it may stick to the pan. Then mix all ingredients together in the pan. Pour in the rosé wine to deglaze the pan. Then add in the tomatoes. Gently use a wooden spatula to break up all the tomato pieces and any remaining chunks of pork. Gently simmer for about 3 minutes or so.

To serve, pour the hot sauce over the cooked spaghetti pasta. Toss gently to coat the pasta evenly. Serve immediately.

Nutritional Content Information
- ➤ Servings 4
- ➤ Calories 686
- ➤ Protein 11
- ➤ Carbs 55
- ➤ Fat 46

Come and cook this recipe along with us at http://www.liveoutyourlight.com

A delightful classic salad that is so attractive as well as nutritional. For added health benefits prepare the salad dressing with apple cider vinegar, instead of balsamic. Your body will thank you.

Spinach and Strawberry Salad

- ♦ ¼ cup unsalted pecans or cashews
- ♦ 5 ounces of fresh baby spinach, triple washed and drained
- ♦ 1-quart ripe strawberries. washed trimmed and sliced

    For the dressing
- ♦ ⅛ apple cider vinegar
- ♦ 2 tsp extra virgin olive oil
- ♦ 1 heaping tsp honey
- ♦ ¼ tsp honey mustard
- ♦ salt and pepper to taste

Take the nuts and grind them in a grinder or food processor. Set aside. Check the leaves of the baby spinach and cut off any unsightly ends. Put the spinach in a large bowl. And add the sliced strawberries. Very gently mix them. Transfer the salad to a serving platter. Sprinkle the nuts on top. Pass the dressing at the table.

Nutritional Content Information
- ➤ Servings 4
- ➤ Calories 239
- ➤ Protein 6
- ➤ Carbs 47
- ➤ Fat 3

Come and cook this recipe along with us at http://www.liveoutyourlight.com

....

To make the dressing proceed as follows

In a medium sized bowl, add in all the ingredients. Whisk until well combined. Taste and adjust the salt and pepper to your liking.

....

Nutritional Content Information
- ➤ Servings 4
- ➤ Calories 20
- ➤ Protein 0
- ➤ Carbs 0
- ➤ Fat 2

This is a double blessing in one recipe. It can be made with canned salmon or fresh salmon. Attaining a very similar taste in flavor without much compromise.

Salmon Fried Rice

- 1-3 Tbsp olive oil
- ⅓ cup corn
- ½ cup well-packed lettuce leaves washed & cut julienne style
- 2 spring onions, green & white thinly sliced
- 2 medium eggs, scrambled and chopped into tiny bits
- 2 cup yield, cooked rice, any variety, from the day before
- 1 tin/115 grams salmon in oil with peppercorns, loosely chopped

Open the salmon tin. Carefully drain out the oil and peppercorns. Set aside. Use a very large sauté pan or wok to heat 1 tsp of the olive oil. When the heat is medium-high add the corn and heat through to scar the corn with the hot oil a bit, about 3 minutes. Then add in the previously cooked rice. Add a tablespoon more of olive oil as needed. Fry the rice for about 7 minutes. It will start to have patches of caramel color due to the frying. Follow with the cooked eggs, the lettuce, and the spring onions. Turn off the heat and gently fold in the salmon. Serve immediately.

Nutritional Content Information
- Servings 4
- Calories 253
- Protein 7g
- Carbs 28g
- Fat 12g

Come and cook this recipe along with us at http://www.liveoutyourlight.com

Pestos are all over Italy. And rightly so. This is a magnificent way to digest nuts in a healthy quantity for most. Even better you can make smokehouse pesto at the beginning of the week. And make honey roasted pesto in the weekend. With such ease!

Honey Roasted Pesto Sauce

- ◆ 1 cup honey roasted almonds or smokehouse brand almonds
- ◆ 3 to 6 dried apricots
- ◆ ½ cup light cheese or cream cheese
- ◆ ½ cup green onion, green & white, loosely chopped
- ◆ ⅓ cup extra virgin olive oil
- ◆ salt & pepper to taste

In a food processor, add in each ingredient at a time. Whiz for a few seconds with each addition. This sauce goes well with cooked pasta, grilled meats, and sandwiches. If you like to get spicy, then add in a half teaspoon or so of cayenne pepper. This sauce may be refrigerated for up to three days.

Nutritional Content Information
- ➤ Servings 4
- ➤ Calories 710
- ➤ Protein 15g
- ➤ Carbs 67g
- ➤ Fat 48g

Come and cook this recipe along with us at http://www.liveoutyourlight.com

This sauce is meant to introduce ginger into your (kids) diet. Start with using the ginger candies. Then as you make this recipe again and again, slowly start to exchange the candies for real fresh minced ginger, for added health benefits. You will have just as many likes and subscribers at your dinner table.

Candied Ginger Sauce

- 8 pieces of ginger chew candies, finely minced
- ½ cup leeks, white part, finely chopped
- ¼ cup golden raisins, finely chopped
- ⅛ cup to ¼ cup vodka
- ¼ cup green onions, thinly sliced
- ½ cup whipping cream
- 2 Tbsp butter or margarine

Take a small bowl and soak the raisins in the vodka. Set aside. Meanwhile, heat the butter or margarine in a sauté pan. Add the leeks and stir continuously for about 7 minutes. The leeks will change in color as they begin to stick to the pan. Then add the raisins soaked in vodka to deglaze the pan. Then add the ginger. Sauté for about 5 minutes more. Turn off the heat. Stir in the whipping cream. Keep stirring the sauce gently until well combined and slightly thickened. Garnish with green onions. This sauce goes well with seared scallops or farfalle pasta.

Nutritional Content Information
- Servings 4
- Calories 237
- Protein 1g
- Carbs 38g
- Fat 9g

Come and cook this recipe along with us at http://www.liveoutyourlight.com

It often concerned me about what to do with the left-over celery sticks. Until I decided to do something about it! And this recipe was born.

Celery and Onion Casserole

- ◆ 6 cups celery, sliced paper thin
- ◆ 1 medium onion, sliced paper thin
- ◆ 1 cup whipping cream
- ◆ ½ cup Parmesan cheese or cheddar cheese
- ◆ 1 Tbsp almond flour
- ◆ 2 Tbsp butter or margarine
- ◆ ¼ Tbsp thyme, dried
- ◆ salt and pepper to taste
- ◆ ¼ cup parsley, chopped

The key to making this a fantastic dish under 20 minutes is slicing the celery and onion paper thin with a food processor. Use a glass baking dish if possible, 9"x13". Preheat oven to 350F/180C. Meanwhile heat the butter or margarine in a large sauté pan over low to medium heat. Add the celery and onions. Season them with salt, pepper, and thyme. So that they wilt slightly about 5 minutes. Turn off the heat. Add in the whipping cream, almond flour, and ⅓ cup of the cheese. Stir gently so that the cheese melts into the cream. Keep stirring until the sauce is evenly distributed around the celery and onion. Adjust seasons if needed now. Pour into the glass baking dish. Bake for 15 minutes. Turn off the oven. After removing the casserole from the oven sprinkle the top with the remaining cheese and fresh parsley. Return to oven to melt the cheese. Serve immediately.

Nutritional Content Information
- ‣ Servings 4
- ‣ Calories 211
- ‣ Protein 6g
- ‣ Carbs 10g
- ‣ Fat 17g

Come and cook this recipe along with us at http://www.liveoutyourlight.com

I can only go a few weeks before I really need to enjoy a bowl of Indian flavors with basmati rice. This is it. For my meat lovers, I add to their plate some cooked meat cubes or cooked meatballs and pour the sauce over it all. Everyone gets happy.

Indian Styled Sauce

- ◆ 2 tsp olive oil
- ◆ 1 white onion, finely chopped
- ◆ 2 cloves garlic, minced
- ◆ 3 Tbsp natural yogurt
- ◆ ½ tsp turmeric
- ◆ 1 tsp garam masala
- ◆ 14-ounce chopped tomatoes
- ◆ salt and pepper to taste
- ◆ Basmati rice to serve

Heat 2 tsp of olive oil in a large sauté pan. Add the onion and garlic and sauté for about 5 minutes until softened. Stir occasionally. Then stir in the turmeric, garam masala, and the yogurt a tablespoon at a time. Then add the tomatoes and the natural juice. Keep the heat on medium and continue to stir the sauce to break up the tomatoes. While stirring, use the wooden spatula to break up the tomatoes. Allow the sauce to bubble. When ready to serve, sprinkle with fresh coriander to garnish. Serve with steamed basmati rice.

Nutritional Content Information
- ➤ Servings 4
- ➤ Calories 81
- ➤ Protein 4g
- ➤ Carbs 13g
- ➤ Fat 3g

Come and cook this recipe along with us at http://www.liveoutyourlight.com

This recipe came out when my son was a little boy. We'd put the spinach balls in a rimmed plate, covered in homemade tomato sauce, and sprinkled with a bit of cheese. Recently my son's teenage friend asked for the recipe. Saying, "it's so good, I want to learn to make them myself".

Spinach Balls in Tomato Sauce

- ◆ 10-ounce fresh or frozen spinach, washed and drained well
- ◆ ½ cup white mild or sharp cheddar, grated
- ◆ ½ cup milk, whole or low fat
- ◆ Add in 1 ½ cups homemade* or boxed biscuit mix
- ◆ salt and pepper taste
- ◆ 1 recipe of tomato sauce, listed on page 24.

Preheat oven to 350F/180C. In a large mixing bowl add biscuit mix, milk, spinach, and grated cheese. Mix well. Add the salt and pepper to taste. Use a cookie sheet tray, lined with parchment paper. Take a heaping tablespoon of the mixture and roll it in the palms of your two hands. Forming a ball. Place it on the cookie sheet tray. Continue until all the mix has been rolled into balls. Keep an inch or so of space between each ball. Place tray in oven and cook for about 8 minutes. And set a timer. Meanwhile, heat the previously made tomato sauce. To prepare for serving, use a dinner plate with a high circular design rim. Spread a thin layer of the tomato sauce inside all of this rim. After timer goes off, check spinach balls. If needed, turn the tray around in the oven and bake for about 5 minutes more. Keep a watchful eye so that they do not burn. Once the spinach balls are ready, place them on top of the plated tomato sauce. Serve additional tomato sauce at the table.

Nutritional Content Information
- ➤ Servings 4
- ➤ Calories 337
- ➤ Protein 10g
- ➤ Carbs 38g
- ➤ Fat 16g

Come and cook this recipe* along with us at http://www.liveoutyourlight.com

The original recipe was made with snake beans. Due to the time, Herriot beans make an excellent stand-in. If you like to serve this as an entree, add about ¾ pound double minced beef or pork before adding the beans. Brown the meat slightly and proceed. *

Drunk Beans Sauce

- 2 tsp olive oil
- 2 cloves garlic, minced
- 1 pd Harriot beans, washed and ends trimmed
- 2 cans/14-ounce chopped tomatoes
- ¼ tsp white sugar
- 1 tsp fresh basil, or ½ dried basil
- ½ cup full-bodied red wine
- salt and pepper to taste
- ¼ cup parsley, chopped
- serve with crusty artisan bread

In a large sauté pan, heat olive oil. * Add Harriot beans and garlic. Sauté for about 3 minutes, stirring constantly. Then add in the tomatoes, sugar, and wine. Then add in all the seasonings. Keep an eye to the sauce while using the wooden spatula to break up the chunks of tomatoes. Adjust with salt and pepper before serving. Garnish with parsley. Serve with slices of crusty artisan bread to soak up the sauce.

Nutritional Content Information
- Servings 4
- Calories 473
- Protein 22g
- Carbs 77g
- Fat 9g

Come and cook this recipe along with us at http://www.liveoutyourlight.com

Such a moist cake that will leave you longing for more. This makes for a luxury and healthy-ish breakfast, afternoon tea, or dessert anytime and anywhere.

Mega Moist Yogurt Cake

Bowl 1
- 1 cup butter or margarine
- 2 cups firmly packed brown sugar
- 1 tsp orange or lemon peel
- 1 tsp vanilla bean extract
- 3 eggs
- 1 tsp zest of lemon or orange, if desired

Bowl 2
- 2 cups almond or whole wheat flour
- ¼ cup wheat germ or more flour
- ¼ tsp baking soda
- ½ tsp salt
- 1 cup plain orange or lemon flavored yogurt

Preheat oven to 350F/180C. In a small bowl beat butter and sugar. Add in finely chopped peel, the zest, if desired, and the vanilla extract. Gently add in the eggs, using a whisk to incorporate them. In another larger bowl, add the flour, wheat germ, baking soda, and salt. Use a baking spatula to mix well. Add the butter mixture (bowl 1) into the flour mixture (bowl 2). Mix well. Then add the yogurt. Pour into mini loaf tins. Fill ¾ full, leaving space for expansion during baking. Bake for 15 minutes. Remove from the oven and insert a toothpick to see if it is done. If needed, turn tin around in the oven and bake a few minutes more. Being careful not to over bake so your cake will remain moist. Remove from tins after baking and allow to cool on a wire rack.

Nutritional Content Information
- Servings 8
- Calories 455
- Protein 5g
- Carbs 58g
- Fat 24g

Come and cook this recipe along with us at http://www.liveoutyourlight.com

This is the foolproof way to *"hit the ball out of the park"* at the next church picnic or country fair. The bonus is you can easily whip up four different flavors to *brag* along.

Muffins for Many

Bowl 1
- ♦ 1 ¾ cup all-purpose flour or almond flour
- ♦ ⅓ cup white sugar
- ♦ 2 tsp baking powder
- ♦ ¼ tsp salt

Bowl 2
- ♦ 1 egg, beaten
- ♦ ¾ cup milk, whole or low-fat
- ♦ ¼ cup cooking oil

Preheat oven to 350F/180C. Line twenty-four mini muffin cups with paper liners. Set aside. In a large bowl, combine flour, sugar, baking powder, and salt. Mix well to incorporate the ingredients. Then form a well in the middle of the mixture. Set aside. In a smaller bowl, combine the egg, milk, and cooking oil. Use a whisk to gently incorporate the ingredients. Add the egg mixture (bowl 2) all at once into the well of the flour mixture (bowl 1). Stir until the mixture is evenly moistened. Batter will still be thick and a bit lumpy.

Choose your flavoring from the following list and stir it into the batter. Pour batter into muffin cups. Filling the cup ⅔ full. (If using streusel topping, then sprinkle it over the muffins now.) Place in oven and bake for 10 minutes. Remove from the oven and insert a toothpick to see if it is done. If needed, turn tin around in the oven and bake a few minutes more. Being careful not to over bake it as it would cause these mini muffins to dry out. Remove from tins after baking and allow cooling on a wire rack.

Come and cook this recipe along with us at http://www.liveoutyourlight.com

Nutritional Content Information
- ➤ Servings 24
- ➤ Calories 41
- ➤ Protein 1g

- ➤ Carbs 3g
- ➤ Fat 3g

....

For Streusel topping proceed as follows.

- ◆ 3 tsp all-purpose flour or almond flour
- ◆ 3 tsp brown sugar
- ◆ ¼ tsp ground cinnamon
- ◆ 2 tsp butter
- ◆ 2 walnuts or pecans, finely chopped

In a small bowl, stir together the flour, brown sugar, and the cinnamon. Then cut in the butter until the mixture resembles coarse crumbs. Stir in the chopped nuts.

....

Nutritional Content Information
- ➤ Servings 24
- ➤ Calories 58
- ➤ Protein 1g

- ➤ Carbs 4g
- ➤ Fat 5g

....

For blueberry muffins proceed as follows.

Prepare basic mix as above, then fold in ¾ cup fresh or frozen blueberries.

....

Come and cook this recipe along with us at http://www.liveoutyourlight.com

Nutritional Content Information
- ‣ Servings 24
- ‣ Calories 46
- ‣ Protein 1g

- ‣ Carbs 5g
- ‣ Fat 3g

....

For lemon muffins proceed as follows.

Prepare basic mix as above, then fold in 2 tsp lemon zest, which has been finely chopped.

....

Nutritional Content Information
- ‣ Servings 24
- ‣ Calories 40
- ‣ Protein 1g

- ‣ Carbs 3g
- ‣ Fat 3g

....

For cheese muffins proceed as follows.

Prepare basic mix as above, then stir in ½ cup shredded cheese, such as sharp cheddar or Monterey Jack cheese.

....

Nutritional Content Information
- ‣ Servings 24
- ‣ Calories 50
- ‣ Protein 1g

- ‣ Carbs 3g
- ‣ Fat 4g

Come and cook this recipe along with us at http://www.liveoutyourlight.com

You can make yourself, and your family easily smile with this. Best yet, whoever washes the dishes can have extra chocolate sauce!

Grilled Pineapple with Chocolate Drizzle

- ◆ 1 small fresh pineapple, peeled, cored, and sliced ⅝ inch thick
  or 1 small can of pineapple slices, liquid drained
- ◆ 4 ounces of dark chocolate, finely chopped
- ◆ ¼ cup walnuts or pecans, finely chopped
- ◆ a few drops of olive oil

To melt the chocolate, you can either use the microwave or the oven. For microwave, place chocolate in a microwave-safe dish and microwave for a few seconds. Carefully remove and set aside. If using the stovetop, take a saucepan and warm over medium heat with a few olive oil drops. When you see that the oil is hot turn off the heat. Stir in the dark chocolate. Stir constantly until completely melted. If you find the chocolate sauce is thick, then add 1 or 2 more drops of olive oil. Set aside. Use a grilling pan or outside BBQ grill. Brush the pineapple slices with olive oil using a pastry brush. And grill for a few minutes to make the char lines appear. Remove from heat.

To serve place pineapple on a dessert plate. Fill the center hole of the pineapple with chocolate sauce. Drizzle additional chocolate sauce around the rim of the plate. Sprinkle with chopped nuts.

Nutritional Content Information
- ➤ Servings 4
- ➤ Calories 361
- ➤ Protein 4g
- ➤ Carbs 67g
- ➤ Fat 12g

Come and cook this recipe along with us at http://www.liveoutyourlight.com

When I first got married, my husband at that time would keep saying, "Can you make pasta frolla?" I later understood he was asking for homemade butter pie crust. Today I answer, yes, I can.

Mini Fruit Tarts

For the Pasta Frolla

- 1 ¼ cup all-purpose flour
- ¼ cup granulated white sugar
- ¼ tsp salt
- ¼ tsp lemon rind, finely minced, optional flavoring
- 3 ounces butter, cut into small pieces
- wax paper

For the Filling

- 12 ounces thick berry marmalade, no added sugar
- 1 egg, beaten and mixed with 1 Tbsp water

If you are short on time, you may prefer to use store-bought readymade pie crust. It will work just as well. Although, you will not enjoy the bragging rights of making tartlets completely by hand.

Preheat oven to 350F/180C. To make the pastry in a bowl or using a food processor, blend together the flour, sugar, salt, and lemon rind, if using. Then cut in the butter with a knife, one piece at a time. If using the food processor method, drop the butter in the safety tube opening of the cover, one piece at a time. Give a whiz for each drop of butter. Slowly add in the milk, about 1 Tbsp at a time. Mix in only enough milk for the dough to hold its' shape. Remove all from the bowl or food processor, and gather into a ball. Wrap the dough in wax paper and refrigerate at least one hour or overnight.

Flour your work surface. Using a pastry roller, roll out the dough to ⅛-inch thick. Using a knife, cut circles for the bottom of your crust. Lay the crust in the tartlet tin. Leave a bit of dough overlapping the edges. So, they can be sealed later. Fill the tartlets evenly with marmalade. Gather up the remaining dough and roll it out to ⅛ inch thick. Cut the circles for the top. Brush the edges of the bottom layer crust with the beaten egg. Place the top layer of dough over the marmalade. Pinch the dough closed to seal it all around. (Crimp the dough in a decorative style if you wish.) Cut a hole in the middle of the dough. You may use a knife or a decorative pastry tool as you wish. Brush the tops of the tartlets with two coats of egg wash. Place tartlets in the oven and bake for 10 minutes. Remove from the oven and check if the crust is done. If not, turn the tartlet pan around and bake for a few minutes more. Being careful not to over bake it. As it would cause these tartlets to dry out. Remove from tins after baking and allow to cool on a wire rack.

Nutritional Content Information
- ➤ Servings 8
- ➤ Calories 107
- ➤ Protein 0g
- ➤ Carbs 7g
- ➤ Fat 9g

This is the day I fell for Rachael Ray. Her common sense, no-frills style of cooking has stayed with me over the years. This is Rachael's recipe, as I heard and wrote it on a napkin. Thank you, dear.

Racheal Rays' Moms' Chocolate Cups

- ◆ 2 cups chocolate baking chips
- ◆ 1 egg
- ◆ 2 Tbsp white granulated sugar
- ◆ 2 Tbsp of your favorite liqueur
- ◆ pinch of salt
- ◆ 1 cup boiling milk

Using a food processor, add in the first five ingredients. Whiz a few seconds to break up the chocolate into a powder-like consistency. Using the safety tube opening cover, carefully and slowly pour the boiling hot milk into the food processor. While on low speed the chocolate mixture will start to turn into a chocolate pudding mixture. Once the mixture is well-incorporated stop the food processor. Using a spatula carefully scrape out the chocolate pudding. Pour into dessert glasses and enjoy immediately or refrigerate for use within three days.

Nutritional Content Information
- ‣ Servings 8
- ‣ Calories 390
- ‣ Protein 7g
- ‣ Carbs 31g
- ‣ Fat 27g

Come and cook this recipe along with us at http://www.liveoutyourlight.com

I often make these mini fruit harvests in the hot summer months. They are well received by children as well as adults.

A Fruit Harvest

- ½ cup gluten-free granola mix
- 5 Tbsp butter, melted
- ¼ cup white granulated sugar
- ½ cup yogurt, any flavor
- ½ cup fresh berries or other fruit of your desire

Preheat oven to 350F/180C. Mini muffin tins may be used. Which will be a yield of twelve. Or regular cupcake tins may be used. Which will be a yield of six. Spray the tins with nonstick baking spray or additional butter. Using a food processor, whiz granola until finely crumbled. Stir in the butter and sugar. Carefully remove the mixture with a spatula. Spoon the mixture into each tin. Pressing the center to form an indentation in the center and rim all around. Bake for 6 to 8 minutes, or until the edges begin to turn slightly golden. Remove from tins and allow to cool on a wire rack. Place a heaping spoonful of yogurt in each. Top with your desired fruits. Serve immediately. Or refrigerate for three days.

Nutritional Content Information
- Servings 12
- Calories 51
- Protein 1g
- Carbs 9g
- Fat 1g

Come and cook this recipe along with us at http://www.liveoutyourlight.com

Occasionally the day goes completely wrong and I get home frustrated and dilapidated about life's events. I must confess I go straight to my freezer for help. I will comfort myself with a cup of tea and a homemade, freshly baked, slice of these chunks of chocolate cookies. (Okay, maybe two...)

Chunks of Chocolate Cookies

- ½ cup honey
- 1 cup packed brown sugar
- 1 ½ tsp baking soda
- ½ tsp salt
- ¾ cup butter, cold
- 2 eggs
- 1 ½ tsp vanilla extract
- 2 cups almond or all-purpose flour
- 1 cup whole wheat flour or almond or all-purpose flour
- ½ cup oat bran or wheat germ or wheat flour
- 1 ½ cups/300 gr 85% dark chocolate bar, cut into chunks, or chocolate chips

In a large bowl mix in the first five ingredients. Taking care that the ingredients are well incorporated. Then proceed to add in the rest of the food ingredients, as listed above. Put a long piece of wax paper on your work surface. Put the dough in the center of wax paper. Shape the dough into a long tube. Use the size diameter of cookie you like. Pull up the horizontal ends of the wax paper and fold over together. This will seal the tube side. Then twist the ends of the wax paper. And seal it with a twist tie. Do this on both ends, like a sausage. Put in the freezer and use within three months.

To serve preheat oven to 350F/180C. Take out the frozen dough. Untie one side and open it well. Carefully, with a large knife, (adult supervision required) slice ¼ inch thick slice and place in on a nonstick baking tray or a parchment-lined tray. Bake for 8 minutes. Remove from the oven and check if the cookie is done. If not, turn the pan around and bake for a few minutes more. Being careful not to over bake it. As it would cause this cookie type to burn. Remove from baking tray after baking and allow to cool on a wire rack.

Come and cook this recipe along with us at http://www.liveoutyourlight.com

Nutritional Content Information
- ❯ Servings 24
- ❯ Calories 117
- ❯ Protein 2g
- ❯ Carbs 23g
- ❯ Fat 9g

Recipe Suitability Guide

	Western Suitable	Asian Suitable	Keto Diet Adaptable	Vegan Adaptable	Crowd Pleaser	Kids Pleaser	Freezable	Sheet Pan Adaptable
Daily Bread	*			*	*	*	*	*
Flat Breads	*	*		*	*	*	*	
BBQ Sauce	*		*	*	*	*	*	*
Sweet Thai (Chile) Sauce	*	*	*	*	*	*		*
Buffalo Sauce	*	*	*	*	*	*		*
Enchilada Sauce	*	*	*	*	*	*	*	*
Jerk Seasoning Mix	*	*	*	*	*	*	*	*
Adobe Seasoning Mix	*	*	*	*	*	*	*	*
Quesadillas	*	*		*		*		
Peanut Sauce	*	*	*	*		*		*
15-Minute Lasagna x3	*	*		*	*	*	*	
Island Styled Chicken	*	*	*			*		
Hot & Spicy Chorizo Chili	*	*			*		*	
Honey Delight Sauce	*	*	*	*	*	*	*	*
Thyme Marinade	*	*	*	*	*	*	*	*
Pesto with Sun Dried Tomatoes	*			*				*
Lemon Braised Broccoli Rabe'	*	*	*	*	*	*		
Ricotta and Bean Pate'	*	*		*	*	*		
Mini Meat Loaves	*		*		*	*	*	*
Portuguese Kale Soup	*	*	*					

Come and cook these recipes along with us at http://www.liveoutyourlight.com Enjoy the full details of each recipe suitability fully explained.

	Western Suitable	Asian Suitable	Keto Diet Adaptable	Vegan Adaptable	Crowd Pleaser	Kids Pleaser	Freezable	Sheet Pan Adaptable
"Mocked Prosciutto di Parma" Sauce for Pasta	*							
An Orange Tree Salad	*	*	*	*	*	*		
Pork Tomato Sauce for Pasta	*							
Spinach & Strawberry Salad	*	*	*	*	*	*		
Salmon Fried Rice	*	*			*	*		
Honey Roasted Pesto Sauce	*		*	*				*
Candied Ginger Sauce	*	*	*	*		*		
Celery & Onion Casserole	*	*	*	*				*
Indian Styled Sauce	*	*	*	*	*	*	*	
Spinach Balls in Tomato Sauce	*	*		*	*	*		*
Drunken Beans Sauce	*	*	*	*	*	*		
Mega Moist Yogurt Cake	*	*			*	*		
Muffins for Many	*	*			*	*		
Grilled Pineapple with Chocolate Drizzle	*	*	*	*		*		
Mini Fruits Tarts	*	*				*		
Racheal Ray's Mom's Chocolate Cups	*	*	*		*	*		
A Fruit Harvest	*	*		*	*	*		
Chunks of Chocolate Cookies	*	*			*	*		*

Come and cook these recipes along with us at http://www.liveoutyourlight.com Enjoy the full details of each recipe suitability fully explained.

Printed in the United States
By Bookmasters